FATHOM BIBLE STUDIES

the wilderness
EXODUS-DEUTERONOMY

DEEP DIVE INTO THE STORY OF GOD

FATHOM: THE WILDERNESS
EXODUS–DEUTERONOMY
LEADER GUIDE

Writer: Lyndsey Medford
Editor: Ben Howard
Designer: Keely Moore

Websites are constantly changing. Although the websites recommended in this resource were checked at the time this unit was developed, we recommend that you double-check all sites to verify that they are still live and that they are still suitable for students before doing the activity.

ISBN: 9781501839238

PACP10510249-01

17 18 19 20 21 22 23 24 25 26 — 10 9 8 7 6 5 4 3 2 1

MANUFACTURED IN THE UNITED STATES OF AMERICA

CONTENTS

About Fathom

Fathom.

It's such a big word. It feels endless and deep. It's the kind of word that feels like it should only be uttered by James Earl Jones with the bass turned all the way up.

Which means it's the perfect word to talk about a God who's infinite and awe-inspiring. It's also the perfect word for a book like the Bible that's filled with miracles and inspiration, but also wrestles with stories of violence and pain and loss.

The mission of *Fathom* is to dive deep into the story of God that we find in the Bible. You'll encounter Scriptures filled with inspiration and encouragement, and you'll also explore passages that are more complicated and challenging.

Each lesson will focus on one passage, but will also launch into the larger context of how God's story is being told through that passage. More importantly, each lesson will explore how God's story is intimately tied to our own stories, and how a God who is beyond our imagination can also be a God who loves us deeply and personally.

We invite you to wrestle with this and more as we dive deep into God's story.

How to Use This Book

First, we want to thank you for teaching this class! While we strive to provide the best material possible for leaders and students, we know that your personal connection with your teens is the most important part of the lesson.

With that out of the way, welcome to the *Fathom Leader Guide*. Each lesson is designed around Kolb's Learning Cycle and moves students through five sections: *Sync, Tour, Reveal, Build,* and *After.*

Sync introduces the students to the general theme of each lesson with a fun activity. There is both a high-energy and low-energy option to choose from in each lesson. *Tour* is the meat of the lesson and focuses intensely on the central Scripture each week. *Reveal* is a time for reflection where youth can digest the information they've heard and start to process it. Then the *Build* section puts this newfound knowledge to practice using creative activities and projects. Finally, *After* gives the students options for practices to try throughout the week to reinforce the central concept of the lesson.

Additionally, before each lesson, a Theology and Commentary section is provided to give you a little more information about the topic being discussed that week.

This Leader Guide is designed to be used hand-in-hand with the *Fathom Student Journal.* Each student will need a journal, and the journals should be kept in the class at the end of the lesson. At the end of the study, give the students their journals as a keepsake to remember what they've learned.

Finally, at the end of this book we've included an Explore More section that offers short outlines for additional lessons if you and your class want to keep diving into these Scriptures after the end of this four-week study.

The Fathom 66 Bible Genre Guid

ENTER ZIP OR LOCATION [＿＿＿＿＿]

Stories ♡
★★★★★
Showtimes: Parts of Genesis, Joshua, Judges, Ruth, 1 Samuel,
2 Samuel, 1 Kings, 2 Kings, 1 Chronicles, 2 Chronicles, Ezra,
Nehemiah, Esther, Matthew, Mark, Luke, John, Acts

The Law ♡
★★★★★
Showtimes: Parts of Genesis, Exodus, Leviticus, Numbers,
Deuteronomy

Wisdom ♡
★★★★★
Showtimes: Job, Some Psalms, Proverbs, Ecclesiastes,
Song of Solomon, Lamentations, James

Psalms ♡
★★★★★
Showtimes: Psalms

The Prophets ♡
★★★★★
Showtimes: Isaiah, Jeremiah, Ezekiel, Hosea, Joel, Amos, Obadiah,
Jonah, Micah, Nahum, Habakkuk, Zephaniah, Haggai, Zechariah,
Malachi

Letters ♡
★★★★★
Showtimes: Romans, 1 Corinthians, 2 Corinthians, Galatians, Ephesians,
Philippians, Colossians, 1 Thessalonians, 2 Thessalonians, 1 Timothy, 2 Timothy,
Titus, Philemon, Hebrews, James, 1 Peter, 2 Peter, 1 John, 2 John, 3 John, Jude

Apocalyptic Writings ♡ TICKETS
★★★★★
Showtimes: Daniel, Revelation

The Fathom Bible Storylines

Create ①

Invite ①

Act Ⓐ

Redeem Ⓡ

Experience Ⓔ

Hope Ⓗ

Introduction to The Wilderness

Background

The four books that follow Genesis describe the beginnings of the Israelite nation. They cover the people's journey from slavery in Egypt to the establishment of their relationship with God in the wilderness to the very doorstep of the land God promised to them. Like Genesis, these books include a number of perspectives that place the story in the context of different experiences with God, giving us a multifaceted depiction of the characters and events at the heart of Israel's origin. At times, this story is a strongly cohesive picture, and at others, the text leaves us with tensions that can be difficult to reconcile.

The beginning of the Exodus story is familiar to churchgoers and moviegoers alike. However, like most Bible stories that make their way into the popular imagination, certain elements tend to get left out in the re-tellings. The second half of Exodus brings us the first of many laws that make up the bulk of these books. Several of the lessons in this study focus on reaching a better understanding of these laws in order to access the untapped spiritual depth in these books. In the law we see, among other things, a way of envisioning a just and beautiful new society under God's leadership.

The Book of Leviticus, which is almost entirely comprised of laws, highlights the beauty and social stability in ordering a nation around precise regulations and religious ceremony. Numbers picks up the narrative threads from the end of Exodus and offers us more insight into the Israelites' development during their time in the wilderness. Finally, we come to Deuteronomy, which is cast as Moses' final speech to the nation before they enter the Promised Land. The laws found here focus more strongly on social justice and warn against forsaking the covenant that the people have made with God.

The story told by these four books and the law that can be found within their pages are, along with Genesis, the foundation of the Jewish faith, and as a result, are the texts that formed Jesus' own religious education. While the world described by these books may appear foreign or even confusing to us, these differences simply give us the opportunity to learn more about what is universal to humankind and help us to appreciate the many different sides of who God is.

The lessons learned by the Israelites in the wilderness are richest when we've done our homework. In order to truly access the meaning of these texts, we must take our time and use commentaries and other resources to find out what archaeologists and biblical scholars say about the context of the words we read. Some of that information will be provided in the following lessons, but we encourage you to continue this quest on your own as well. For now, you're invited on an adventure into another land and another time on a quest to discover more about our own journeys with God.

Fathom Strategy for Reading and Understanding the Bible

"The Bible is written for us, but not to us."

This where we start on our quest. When we read the Bible, we have to constantly remember that the Bible is written for us, but not to us. Understanding the original context of the Bible helps us ask the right questions when interpreting Scripture.

For the first steps in our process, we need to understand how each passage we read functions in context and examine the historical background. When we read a passage, we should ask questions about the era, location, and culture of the original audience, as well as how a particular writing relates to the larger narrative of the Bible. This strategy not only helps us understand a passage's primary meaning, it also gives us guidance on how to translate that meaning into our specific circumstances today.

FATH●M
Moses Sees God

Summary

Students will learn about the Israelites' deliverance from Egypt and God's demonstrations of God's power. Moses' vision of God's glory will also be instructive as the students learn that we always see God incompletely.

Overview

- **Sync** with what students already know about God's self-revelation in Exodus.
- **Tour** through the story of Exodus as the ancient Israelites might have heard it.
- **Reveal** what facets of God emerge in the Exodus narrative by discussing in a small group.
- **Build** on the discussion by exploring different avenues of prayer and worship.
- **After** the lesson, ask the students to choose an activity that will help them continue to learn more about who God is.

Anchor Point

- Exodus 33:19-20—*The LORD said, "I'll make all my goodness pass in front of you, and I'll proclaim before you the name, 'The LORD.' I will be kind to whomever I wish to be kind, and I will have compassion to whomever I wish to be compassionate. But," the LORD said, "you can't see my face because no one can see me and live."*

Supplies

- Student Journals
- Craft and costume supplies (such as cardboard, cans, jugs, toilet paper, paper plates, bowls, cups, straws, construction paper, glue, old T-shirts, blankets)
- Index cards
- Pens and pencils
- Flip charts or posterboard
- Markers and paint
- Optional: small prizes

Parent E-mail

This week we are studying the Book of Exodus and focusing on the attributes of God that are revealed throughout the Israelites' flight from Egypt. The students will consider God's role in this story and will engage with these facets of God through prayer and worship. Here are some ways to engage:

- Ask your youth what aspect of God stood out to them when considering this week's lesson.
- Watch a movie about the Exodus story and talk with your student about how God is portrayed.

Leader Notes

The fact that a "diverse crowd" joined the Israelites as they left Egypt tells us that, even more than their shared ancestry, the moment of the Exodus is the moment that defines the people of Israel going into the future. Following centuries of captivity, they are becoming reacquainted with the God who rescues them from their suffering. For students who may be renegotiating their own relationships with God, this story may not only be instructive, but comforting as they witness God's faithfulness throughout. This lesson will encourage them to see God in new ways, just as the Israelites did in the Exodus.

Theology and Commentary

Compared to the many stories in Genesis that show God in close proximity with humanity and often acting in human-like ways, the Book of Exodus shows us a God whose foremost attributes are power and glory. The Hebrew word for *glory*, "kavod," literally translates as weightiness; it represents the awesome splendor, deep honor, and fullness of God's being.

Perhaps we get our best sense of this concept from Moses' encounter with the burning bush. Moses predicts that the Hebrews, who have lived for years in a polytheistic nation, will ask for the name of the particular god who has sent him. God's response, "I Am Who I Am," does not merely claim that God is the highest and mightiest god or even the only god, but that God exists eternally according to God's own will; that God exists on a plane far beyond the mythological antics of polytheistic gods. This greatness and beyond-ness, God's *kavod*, continues to be manifested throughout Exodus as fire, cloud, smoke, and thunder as God travels with the Israelites.

Still, this awesome God is not only powerful and strong, this God is also compassionate and loving, "hearing the cry of grief" from the Israelites in captivity. In contrast to the oft-capricious behavior of the other deities worshipped in the Ancient Near East, God does not send the ten plagues merely to display power or extort obedience, but on behalf of God's oppressed people.

The Israelites, who begin the book being forced to drown their young boys, eventually see Pharaoh's own men, along with their chariots, drowned. They then turn toward the dry and dusty wilderness, and beyond that, the Promised Land. It is an odd scene. The Israelites who have known only one way of life, slavery, have been hurried out of their homes.

Now they face down the desert with little but the jewelry thrust upon them by the Egyptians. This disconcerted and displaced people will struggle to follow Moses or trust God, but they will remain God's covenant people nonetheless.

The glory and the compassion of God are both demonstrated in Exodus 33. God has threatened to leave the Israelites after the golden calf incident. Moses, who was once fearful and confused by God's call to lead, intercedes on their behalf. He reminds God of God's commitment to the patriarchs and God's care for the people.

Moses, in need of reassurance himself, asks to see God's glory. It's clear that Moses does not know the magnitude of what he's asking for, yet God is gracious. We see in God's actions both intimacy and transcendence. God wants to be known, and creates the conditions under which Moses' request can be granted. At the same time, God is not only incomprehensible, but can barely even be glimpsed. With the palm of God's hand, God tenderly shields Moses from God's glory. Even those most intimate with God can only be invited to see God's features indistinctly, moving away, toned down, but even this glimpse causes Moses' face to radiate with God's glory.

Leader Reflection

Throughout all four years of college, I performed as part of the school's improv team. In my senior year, the group made it a priority to gather all the newest members for a long storytelling session. It was important to us who had a sense of connection to the events and people that had been a part of the team before they arrived. The stories explained why we did things the way we did—how we had come to the values we prioritized as a group and expressed our identity as a team.

It's natural for groups of people to tell their origin stories. The story told in Exodus, though, is a little different. It's not about Israel's great triumphs or even its great faithfulness. In the Exodus story, God alone is triumphant, and that is what we are urged to remember the many times this story is recounted throughout the Bible.

We might not immediately think of this book when we think about our own origin stories, but we, too, are a people called to follow God. Many of us vacillate between seeing ourselves in Moses, God's faithful confidant, and an uncomfortable kinship with the Israelites, easily distracted and whiny. But the focus of the Exodus narrative remains on God. It is God who constitutes our identity as a people.

As teenagers are formulating their own identities and coming into their own understanding of who God is, diving into this story can be an important resource. Its insistence on God's power and faithfulness ground us in these truths, while other elements of the story invite questions and free our imaginations. As you prepare for this lesson, pray that God would help your students connect with this story and with God.

NOTES

SYNC (10-15 minutes)

High-Energy Option—Pictures of God

[Place a variety of craft and costume supplies in the middle of the room. Divide the students into groups of three.]

ASK: What do you think of when you think of God? An old man? A cloud? When you pray, what do you envision? Take a minute to make a list in your Student Journal.

[Give the students about a minute to think, a little longer if they seem to need more time.]

SAY: With your group, agree on three images that you commonly associate with God, and dress up each group member to represent one of those images. You'll have ten minutes to decide and put your costumes together using what you have here. Then we'll share our creations.

[Give the students ten minutes to create their costumes. Have one member from each group explain them.]

ASK: God tells the Israelites not to make any images of God, yet we all have something in mind when we think of God. Why do you think God gave the commandment not to make these visions into physical realities?

[Allow for a few answers from the students and push them to think about both the temptation of idolatry and the idea that God can't be limited to a single representation.]

SAY: In Exodus, the Israelites "meet" God for the first time. In our reading today, pay attention to the images, qualities, and names of God.

Low-Energy Option—Exodus Miniseries

[Divide the students into groups of three or four. Give each group ten index cards.]

SAY: For this game, we're going to review what we already know about the Exodus story, whether it's from Sunday school, movies, or anything else. Imagine you're in charge of the newest TV miniseries based on the Book of Exodus. Come up with five episodes for the series. For instance, one episode could be about Moses and the burning bush. On one index card, write a creative title for the episode. On the other, draw a costume or set for the episode and cast the main characters. Keep the titles in one stack and the episode attributes in another. You'll have about ten minutes.

[Give the students ten minutes to plan their miniseries.]

SAY: Now shuffle up your stacks and switch cards with another group, but don't look at the cards until I say so. You'll have four minutes to match the episodes with their titles. Go!

[Give the groups four minutes to match the cards. The first team to finish wins.]

SAY: Choose a representative from the team you switched with to check your team's answers.

[Once they've checked the answers and determined they're right, crown a winner or give small prizes to every team that got all of their answers correct.]

TOUR (15-20 minutes)

SAY: One of the many reasons we read Scripture out loud during worship is that this is the way it was originally meant to be experienced. Today we're going to hear a large portion of the story of Exodus. For this reading, I'll need three strong, dramatic readers to share the story.

[Choose three readers, and invite them to the front.]

SAY: Our readers are going to guide us through an overview of the whole Exodus story. The journey is a long one, and it might be hard to sit through. But as you listen, imagine that you live in the ancient world where storytelling is one of the main forms of entertainment.

SAY: Think about this as if we're the story of your people. The events we're about to hear are defining moments for the Israelites. The descendants of Joseph were enslaved in Egypt because the Egyptians feared them. In this story, they encounter God who proceeds to rescue them.

SAY: As you listen, focus on this question: What does this story say about God? To stay engaged with the story, write down words or phrases that stand out to you, especially attributes of God shown or described in the reading.

[Have Reader One read excerpts from Section 1—Exodus 3.]

ASK: If you had to give a five-word summary of what just happened, what would it be?

[Allow for two or three responses. Then have the readers read Section Two from the Student Journal.]

ASK: What would be your five-word summary of these passages?

[Allow for two or three responses from different students than before. Then have the readers read Section Three.]

ASK: What words did you write down that stuck out to you from this passage?

SAY: When Moses encountered the burning bush earlier, God said that the people would come back and worship on Mount Sinai. Do you think this is what we were supposed to envision?

[Allow for a few responses, then have all three readers finish reading the passages from Section Four.]

SAY: Give our readers a round of applause! Thank you so much for that.

REVEAL (10 minutes)

[Ask the students to gather in groups of three or four to discuss the questions in the Student Journal.]

SAY: Use the questions in your Student Journal to discuss the story we just heard. I'll be moving from group to group to see how you're doing and if you have any questions about the story.

[Give the students ten minutes to discuss the questions. As they do, travel around to the groups and ask what questions they've written during their discussion. Take note of the questions and look up answers later, if necessary.]

Journal Questions

- What attributes of God did you hear in the story? Where have you seen these demonstrated in other parts of the Bible or in your own experience?
- What questions did you have about the story?
- Are you more likely to imagine God on a fiery, thunderous mountain or gently hiding someone in a safe place? hearing the cries of God's people or wrathfully punishing their oppressors? What images, feelings, and questions come up when you hold all of these images and stories together?

BUILD (10-15 minutes)

[Before the lesson, set up the following stations around the room:
Prayer Station: posterboard, markers, and a prayer book;
Song Station: posterboard, markers, guitar (optional);
Dance Station: large empty space;
Art Station: posterboard, paint, markers.]

SAY: There is always more to discover about God, and the best way to gain that understanding is to talk to God directly! After discussing the attributes and actions of God, we are going to move into a time of prayer and worship together. Think about the form you'd like to use to express your worship toward God. You'll be able to choose between creating a prayer, a song, a dance, or a painting.

SAY: Once you choose which station you want to work at, you'll work with the others who chose that station and take some time to bring together your ideas, your questions, your prayers, and your praises to create something together.

SAY: You may want to start by focusing on an attribute of God that is demonstrated in Exodus as the theme of your creation. It may be a little different to think of some of these activities as forms of prayer, but don't worry—you only need to create something between your group and God; you won't have to share with the rest of the class.

[Go around the room to demonstrate where each activity will take place, and give the students a chance to pick which of the stations they prefer. Allow the students ten to fifteen minutes to put together their creation. As they work, travel around the room and ask groups questions to help them stay on task and work through the prayerful aspect of this activity.]

ASK: What attributes of God did you discuss as a team? Which ones did you decide to focus on?

ASK: Does your creation focus mostly on worship, prayer, asking questions, or something else? Why did you decide to move in this direction?

ASK: Does it feel strange to *(insert activity)* as a form of prayer? How does thinking about it as prayer change the way you are engaging in it?

[After each group is done, bring the group back together and ask some of these questions to the group as a whole, allowing them to share their reflections in light of what they've created.]

AFTER (5 minutes)

[Invite the students to participate in an After activity. Send them a reminder during the week.]

Probing Questions

SAY: This week ask a friend or family member what attributes of God have stood out to them in their life recently. Share with them an attribute you noticed in today's lesson that connected with you.

Continue the Conversation

SAY: Write a letter to me or another one of your youth leaders that includes one of the questions raised by our lesson this week. We might not have the answer, but we might be able to share a story or some insight. Set up a time to talk with one of us about your question.

Constant Reminders

SAY: Write down one of the attributes of God that most intrigued or inspired you today. Ask God to show you this week more of this attribute. Whenever something reminds you of that word or quality, take a picture of it and post it on social media.

PRAYER

SAY: Together, let's recite the following prayer.

God, we thank you for the many ways you reveal yourself to us so that we can be in relationship with you. Let us see the signs of your presence with us and work in the world this week. Amen.

God's Laws Set God's People Apart

Summary

Students will learn about the laws in Leviticus and contemplate the purposes of these laws: to benefit God's people, to set them apart from their neighbors, and to remind them of their covenant to be holy. Students will also learn the importance obedience serves as an invitation to greater freedom.

Overview

- **Sync** with the way that laws build a society through a creative activity.
- **Tour** through Leviticus 19 and its historical context as an entry point in discussing the law.
- **Reveal** the students' personal thoughts about Leviticus 19 through a devotional activity.
- **Build** on the concept of holiness through illustration.
- **After** the lesson, choose an activity that will help the students put their thoughts about holiness into practice.

Anchor Point

- Leviticus 19:1-2—*The LORD said to Moses, Say to the whole community of the Israelites: You must be holy, because I, the LORD your God, am holy.*

Supplies

- Student Journals
- Paper
- Markers or coloring supplies
- A hat
- Flip chart

Parent E-mail

This week we're investigating a little-appreciated part of the Bible, the Book of Leviticus. By reading from the law and learning about its historical context, your student will think about how God calls us to holiness and doesn't simply give us a list of arbitrary rules. Here are some ways to connect with your teen this week:

- Invite your student to talk about a household rule they dislike. Ask them why think it exists and invite them, if appropriate, to suggest other rules or habits that might accomplish the same goal.
- Brainstorm with your student about a simple daily habit that will remind your family of God's Word.

Leader Notes

Teenagers tend to have a complicated relationship with rules. At some point, they all tend to come into conflict with rules or boundaries. At the same time, it can be a relief to have a rule or authority figure take the fall for restricting them from something they, in reality, don't want to do at all. Still, they can often see that the adults in their lives find it easier to enforce rules than to demonstrate and instill character. Today's lesson will help the students think about the relationship between the two.

Theology and Commentary

Parts of Leviticus are nearly impenetrable for us today. Long, repetitive lists of instructions for slaughtering and sacrificing animals, inspecting skin diseases, or dealing with bodily discharges are no one's idea of interesting, let alone spiritual, literature. But this book, sitting at the center of the Torah, not only invites us into the historical world of the Israelites, it also demonstrates some of the overriding concerns of that ancient community.

In Leviticus 19 we see a fairly representative list of laws that, while evincing several different purposes, together serve to set Israel apart as God's chosen and holy people. The opening statement makes this clear: "You must be holy, because I, the LORD your God, am holy." The repetition of "I am the LORD" throughout this chapter echoes this statement and offers an example of how repetition was a central element of Hebrew literature.

The many detailed laws show how Israel is outwardly different from their neighbors and also reminds the people throughout each day, month, and year that their lives are ordered by and oriented around God. The laws are not meant to be burdensome, but to mark out the values of the community, creating a sense of belonging, order, and distinctiveness.

Verses 9-18 clearly describe ways the Israelite nation should ensure that justice is done. The poor, travelers, and the disabled are protected, while manipulative and unfair behaviors are prohibited. In contrast to our modern emphasis on individualism, there's a strong sense throughout this passage that the people are responsible for one another. Beyond the specifics offered here, the section ends on the broader command we are all familiar with: "You must love your neighbor as yourself."

The following verses are a bit more confusing and include the somewhat famous prohibition against mixing fabrics. Why would God be concerned with such a thing? These verses reflect a penchant for order and categorization that prizes distinction and separation between things of different kinds. This dovetails with the preoccupation with "clean" and "unclean" elements throughout the law. In addition, these laws are a reminder that distinctions, once compromised, can be difficult to maintain, and that the people should be wise about the ways they, as a holy people, interact with the world.

The final verses in Leviticus 19 remind us again that justice is one of the key markers of a holy people. This extends from small things, like physically showing respect to elders, to general principles, such as dealing honestly with neighbor and stranger alike. All of these behaviors are envisioned as part of an integrated life of holiness.

The laws found here are often challenging and force us to exercise our skills in scriptural interpretation more than other more straightforward books. What modern practices can we enact to remind ourselves to value our elderly? What does it mean to be responsible for our neighbors in a global society? Though its language may be foreign to us, the values and principles set forth in Leviticus continue to challenge us today.

Leader Reflection

If you ask all of your students what they hope their lives will be like, it is unlikely that any of them will immediately respond that they dream of living a life of holiness. In fact, depending on their exposure to media, history, and the church, they may recoil at that word. Too often Christian attempts to pursue holiness have mutated into a "holier-than-thou" prohibition of anything from playing cards to rock n' roll to left-handedness. For many, it's easy to equate the call to holiness with this prohibitive and self-righteous tradition.

Many Christians have been led to read the levitical laws in a similar light. Some are left with the impression that the laws which governed a nation for hundreds of years have never had any purpose but to serve as a lesson in obedience. This leaves us with an impoverished understanding of the Israelite community and a weak argument for holiness in our own community. We should, instead, see the laws—and the concept of holiness—as invitations into a distinct, harmonious, and beautiful way of life.

Leviticus 19, then, is part of God's call to practice disciplines that foster shalom, the deep peace and well-being that is meant to characterize God's people and their society. When we read the law in this light, we can begin to ask what habits and characteristics might continue to make a people holy today so that we can heed the Spirit's gentle call to growth and shalom.

As you prepare for the lesson today, ask God to help you and your students pursue holiness in the light of God's grace, not making an idol of the law, but treasuring it as a lens through which we can see God's will for us.

NOTES

SYNC (10-15 minutes)

High-Energy Option—Gotcha!

[Gather everyone in a circle. Bring a hat that can be passed around the circle.]

SAY: This game is called, "Gotcha!" There are two rules. First, when you're wearing the hat, it's your turn to make up a sound and a motion. Second, after the person with the hat shares their creation, everyone else will repeat it.

(Demonstrate by punching a fist into the air while yelling, "Kapow!" and have the class copy you.)

SAY: There's one more element to this game. After everyone repeats your motion and before you pass the hat to the next person, you'll make up one new rule that will remain in place until the end of the game. If you see someone violate any rule, yell, "Gotcha!" then say the rule they violated. The winner will be the last person to follow all the rules.

[Start the game yourself. Go around the circle as many times as necessary for one person to be left standing.]

SAY: That got difficult pretty quickly, didn't it? How did you feel about the rules by the end?

[Let the students give a few responses.]

SAY: Sometimes this is the way we think about the law in the Old Testament—arbitrary and burdensome. But the laws of Leviticus are more than that; they describe the habits that would help people form a godly society. Today we're going to explore what that means.

Low-Energy Option—Ten More Commandments

[Before the lesson, write each of the following categories on a piece of flip chart paper: Food, Living Arrangements, Holidays, Relationships, Money, Justice, Other.]

ASK: Why do laws exist?

[Allow for a few answers. Help the students talk about how we want to live together as a society.]

SAY: Let's imagine that we're all moving to an island together to form a new nation. We need to make a few rules to govern our society. First, talk to your neighbor about what values these rules should be based on. Use the questions in the Student Journal as a springboard.

[Give the students a few minutes to discuss.]

SAY: Okay, together we're going to make the laws for our society. We'll go through the categories listed here, and you can call out any rule you want made in that category. Then we'll all vote.

[Work through the categories. Write down the rules that are voted into law. Encourage the students to mix up silly laws (Thou shalt only eat tacos on Tuesday) and serious laws. If needed, ask the questions in the Student Journal.]

ASK: How do you like our new society? What kind of society do you think it will be?

[Allow for a few responses.]

SAY: Today we're going to look at the laws God gave the Israelites.

TOUR (20 minutes)

ASK: What do you think of when you hear the word "law"?

[Encourage the students to give answers from secular contexts as well as ideas about the biblical law.]

ASK: I want to know everyone's answer on this question: What does the Bible say about the law?

[Try to get answers from as many students as possible, even if multiple answers are similar. If the group is large, get a show of hands after each answer to find out how many people had similar ideas.]

SAY: The best way to understand the law is to dig in and read it. Today we're going to dive into Leviticus 19, which is a big list of short rules. You can think of it as a sample of the rest of the book. But first, I need everyone to get together in groups of three or four.

[Give the students a moment to organize themselves into groups.]

SAY: Each of your groups is going to go through this entire chapter. Take turns reading a verse each as you move through the chapter. As each verse is read, make a little note about it—you can use symbols like smiley faces, question marks, or anything else that captures your thoughts and feelings.

[Give the students about ten minutes to read through the chapter together.]

SAY: When your group is done, go back and discuss the most interesting, confusing, or compelling laws you read. What do you think their purpose might be?

[Give the students another few minutes to discuss what they've read in their groups.]

ASK: What did you all think? Shout out some of the laws that you thought were the most interesting.

[Repeat answers as the students shout them out to acknowledge them and make sure everyone hears.]

SAY: Usually when Congress makes a new law, the purpose is pretty clear, but that's not exactly the case here. We can understand the laws better when we know the historical context and when we think about what kind of society these laws would help create. In this chapter, we see that most of the laws either benefit God's people, set them apart from their neighbors, or remind them of their obligation to be a community of justice. The last one is probably the easiest to understand from our perspective.

ASK: Look at your Student Journal again. Which of these laws is put in place to protect vulnerable people? Who does it protect?

[Affirm student responses and help them name the categories of people (i.e. the poor, immigrants, and so forth).]

ASK: One of the other categories was laws that would benefit the people. These might not be as clear. Does anyone have a guess at which laws fit here?

[Listen to student responses. Point out any laws they've missed: the command to eat all sacrificed meat within two days has clear health implications; there are obvious benefits in a society for honesty and compassion; the rules about fruit trees are a way of handing down farming wisdom, as the fruit trees grow better when left alone for a few years after they're planted.]

ASK: Finally, as the introduction to Leviticus 19 says, these laws are designed to make the Israelites holy, or set apart. Many of these practices would make them a peculiar people among their neighbors, and their actions would regularly point their attention back to God. Which of these laws seems to be specially designed for this purpose?

[Affirm student responses and push them to point out what these laws imply about holiness. Be sure to explain the most confusing laws: rules about keeping animals and fabrics separate correspond with an ordered lifestyle where things stay in place where they belong; the paragraph about blood, tattoos, beards, and dead spirits refers to the religious practices of neighboring nations that the Israelites were forbidden to adopt because it would lead them away from God.]

SAY: When we look at the purpose these laws served, we can see more than a list of arbitrary rules. Instead, it's a vision for a community that would honor God and flourish as a result. In our next activity, we'll think about what that vision looks like today.

REVEAL (8-10 minutes)

[Have the students get back into their groups.]

SAY: In your Student Journals, you'll find a few Bible passages listed. I'm going to assign one passage to each group. As a group, you're going to practice a variation on a method of Scripture reading that has been used for many centuries. The purpose of this process is to help us listen to what the Holy Spirit is saying through Scripture.

SAY: First, a member of your group will read the passage slowly out loud while the group listens. Then you'll have a minute or two of silence to think and pray about what you've heard. Go ahead and do this first step.

[Once everyone has finished reading and is silent, wait about a minute before continuing.]

SAY: Good job, everybody! The next step is similar. A different member of your group will read the passage slowly and out loud again. Once they're done, read through the passage again silently. Look for a word or phrase that stands out to you. When you've encountered one, say it out loud to the group.

[Give the students a similar amount of time as you did for the first step.]

SAY: Finally, have a third person in your group read the passage out loud one more time. When they're done, share how one of the words or phrases connected with you.

BUILD (10-15 minutes)

SAY: Now that we've discussed it some, I want you to draw what holiness means to you. You might think about the Holy of Holies in the temple or the different ways you've seen the law interpreted. As you're drawing, talk with your group about the discussion questions in your Student Journal.

[Give the students about six or seven minutes to draw their conception of holiness.]

SAY: Let's get back together as a class. Who wants to share what they drew?

[Allow a few students to share their drawings. Ask them to explain why they drew what they drew.]

ASK: What are some examples of ways that it's important for Christians to be set apart? What aspects of "the way things are done" in the wider culture contradict the values God has in mind for us?

[Allow for a few responses. Try to get students involved who don't normally respond.]

ASK: What is your vision of a community that honors God and flourishes?

[Allow for a few responses.]

SAY: The Israelites are commanded to put the words of the law on their doorframes, on their wrists, and to always keep holiness in mind. This week I challenge you to put your holiness drawing on your bathroom mirror or somewhere you'll see it every day.

AFTER (5 minutes)

[Invite the students to participate in one of the After activities. Send them a reminder during the week.]

Modern Doorposts

SAY: Sit down with your family and brainstorm a creative way to add a Scripture or symbol of holiness to a prominent place in your home.

Habits of Holiness

SAY: Talk to a partner about a practice you can adopt this week to remind you to follow God's way rather than adopting the assumptions of the world around you. Text your partner during the week to ask them how their practice is going.

Political Posts

SAY: The next time you hear about a political debate, think about how each position compares with God's vision for society. Share a photo or a Bible verse that relates to this vision on social media.

PRAYER

SAY: Let's all say the following prayer from Psalms together.

I get up in the middle of the night to give thanks to you
because of your righteous rules.
I'm a friend to everyone who honors you
and to all who keep your precepts.
LORD, the world is full of your faithful love!
Teach me your statutes!

Amen.

FATH●M
God's People in the Wilderness

Summary

Students will learn about the circumstances that led to the Israelites' wandering in the wilderness and will reflect on God's discipline. They will discover that the Israelites needed time to change, grow, and learn about God before they could fulfill their destiny in the Promised Land.

Overview

- **Sync** with the experience of wandering around with no ultimate purpose.
- **Tour** through a pivotal moment in the wilderness through a student-led skit.
- **Reveal** what the wilderness means to your students through a journal activity.
- **Build** on the wilderness story by exploring the events that led up to it.
- **After** the lesson, help the students choose an activity that will remind them of God's unseen work in deserted places.

Anchor Point

- Deuteronomy 8:3-5—*He humbled you by making you hungry and then feeding you the manna that neither you nor your ancestors had ever experienced, so he could teach you that people don't live on bread alone. No, they live based on whatever the LORD says. During these forty years, your clothes didn't wear out and your feet didn't swell up. Know then in your heart that the LORD your God has been disciplining you just as a father disciplines his children.*

Supplies

- Student Journals
- Students' smartphones (one per Scavenger Hunt group)
- Props for actors in skit (see Tour for more details)

Parent E-mail

This week's lesson centers on God "sentencing" the Israelites to forty years wandering in the desert. We'll explore what led to this point and why it was necessary to prepare a new generation to inhabit the Promised Land. Here are some ways to engage this week:

- Ask your teen how you think his or her generation will do church differently from yours.
- Research prayer labyrinths (walking paths for prayer) in your area and take your family to one. Discuss your wandering experience over ice cream or another treat.
- Ask your youth if they remember a time when having to wait for something they wanted turned out to be good for them.

Leader Notes

Moses, David, and Jesus all spent time in the wilderness before they were fully equipped to follow God and lead God's people. Teenagers often experience similar situations, but adults run the risk of minimizing the pain and confusion of students as the mere throes of adolescence. Today's lesson attempts to acknowledge the reality of the wildernesses that students experience and helps them put these experiences into perspective.

Theology and Commentary

Throughout the Books of Exodus and Numbers we have seen that the Israelites are slow to trust God. Even before they left Egypt, when their brick-making straw was taken away, they complained against Moses and God's plan. Even after they left Egypt and experienced God's provision in the wilderness, they repeatedly lose trust in God with the appearance of a new hardship or the first sign of discomfort.

Now that they have arrived at the edge of the Promised Land, which should be cause for rejoicing after the spies return with reports land is as bountiful as promised, the people are still unable to trust in God. Despite the bounty they found, the spies convince the Israelites to fixate on the discouraging aspect of their report: the great size of the people and warriors in Canaan. The spies describe these inhabitants as the mythical offspring of gods and humans, and argue that they cannot be defeated.

Caleb and Joshua do not deny the report of their fellow spies, but insist that the people, with God by their side, can and will prevail. Despite the confidence of Caleb and Joshua, the people despair and threaten to return to Egypt. Though Moses and Aaron fall on their faces in supplication begging the people not to resist God's commands, the people are insistent that they will not fight for the land they have been promised.

This chapter is among the episodes in the Bible where one person pleads for the lives of the rest. God appears to be fed up with the Israelites and threatens to wipe them out, but Moses reminds God of God's own words which God proclaimed before Moses on Mount Sinai: "The Lord is very patient and absolutely loyal, forgiving wrongs and disloyalty. Yet he doesn't forgo all punishment, disciplining the grandchildren and great-grandchildren for their ancestors' wrongs" (Numbers 14:18).

God relents. Instead of starting over with Moses' descendants, God will continue the covenant and give the land to the next generation of Israelites. In the meantime, God notes that the children pay for their parents' sin by wandering in the desert for forty years.

The first generation of Israelites to leave Egypt suffers from such a lack of imagination that they would rather return to their subjugation than face hardship on the way to abundance. They repeatedly conclude that they prefer slavery by the Nile to wandering in the desert. Ironically, this attitude leads to decades of wandering in the desert.

The Books of Numbers and Deuteronomy often claim that the people are most tempted to rebel against God when they are comfortable and well-fed. The fact that the children who grew up in the desert will be the ones to faithfully enter the Promised Land appears to confirm this idea further.

Leader Reflection

A long period spent wandering in the wilderness is a theme in many Bible stories. Moses, David, Elijah, and Jesus, among others, were either driven or chose to leave the comfort and safety of their normal lives to spend time in the desert. Several generations of Christians, often called the "desert fathers and mothers," have even followed suit.

The wilderness is not only a dangerous and unforgiving landscape, it's also rather boring. We may hear about one or two isolated moments during these wilderness periods, but our biblical heroes did not go to the wilderness in search of great and exciting things. The wilderness is a place of quiet preparation, simplicity, and God's provision.

You would imagine that the people who had witnessed the ten plagues and the parting of the Reed Sea would be predisposed to the kind of trust necessary to follow God through the wilderness into the Promised Land. Yet, the Israelites remained fearful. Indeed, it was eventually the children of this first generation, raised on the daily miracle of manna, who would follow God's instructions and take the land given to them. In this story, we come to see that there is wisdom in God's discipline. The people need this time in the wilderness to shed the influences of Egypt and to become reacquainted with the God who delivered them.

As many spiritual writers have noted, the wilderness can be a strange gift. These are difficult, yet necessary experiences. For youth, this can be difficult to see in the midst of trying spiritual, social, or relational experiences. It is our task to help them understand that growth is sometimes slow and often painful. As you prepare for this lesson, pray that God will give you and your students strength and patience to be faithful during the times you are in the wilderness.

NOTES

SYNC (10-15 minutes)

High-Energy Option—Photo Scavenger Hunt

[Divide the students into teams of three or four.]

SAY: Today we're going to have a scavenger hunt. For each item on the list in your Student Journal, you must take a photo to prove you've found it. In parentheses beside the item, you'll see what your picture should look like. Make sure you complete the list in order. You'll have ten minutes. Ready? Go!

Scavenger Hunt Items

1) Something that would fit in your shoe *(picture: the item in someone's shoe)*
2) Somewhere a group member has slept before *(picture: the group member sleeping there)*
3) A Bible verse as a decoration *(picture: your whole team pointing at it)*
4) A stuffed animal *(picture: on someone's shoulders)*
5) A paper clip, an eraser, a pen, and some thumbtacks *(picture: make an animal or robot out of them)*
6) A drawing of a biblical character *(picture: someone dancing with the drawing)*
7) A place you're not supposed to bring coffee *(picture: someone pretending to drink coffee there)*
8) A microphone *(picture: your group posing for an album cover)*
9) Five different Bibles *(picture: a building constructed out of them)*
10) The church's comfiest chair *(picture: two group members fighting over it)*

[Walk around with the students. If you have a larger building, make sure you have volunteers available to help supervise the scavenger hunt. After ten minutes, call your students back to the classroom.]

ASK: How did it go? Did you find everything?

SAY: I'm sure some of you were probably wondering if there would be a prize if you finished the whole list, or at least for the team that finished with the most pictures. But . . . surprise, there's not! Your prize today is the experience of wandering around! Today we're going to talk about how that experience can be one of those blessings no one asks for, but we all need.

Low-Energy Option—Desert Songs

[Divide the students into groups of three or four.]

SAY: I want to hear what you all already know about the Israelites in the wilderness. Your group is going to pick a familiar song—maybe a pop song, an old classic, a children's song—and change the words to be about the Israelites' experience in the wilderness. You can look through the end of Exodus and the Book of Numbers if you need inspiration. You'll have about ten minutes to write two verses and a chorus, and then your group will sing the song together.

[Give the students about ten minutes. If you have the capability, find out what songs each group is adapting and pull up karaoke versions on YouTube to accompany their performances.]

SAY: All right, let's hear what everyone has to offer!

[Invite groups up one at a time to sing for everyone.]

SAY: Those were all amazing, and I'm sure some of you are wondering if there will be a prize for the best song, but . . . there's not. Your prize today is the experience of wandering through the Israelites' story. Today we're going to talk about that story and how the biggest blessings can be the things we don't ask for, but desperately need.

TOUR (20 minutes)

SAY: Before the Israelites could go into the Promised Land, they had to scope it out and see what they were dealing with. Moses sent twelve spies, one from each tribe. Today we're going to pick up the story at the end of Numbers 13, when the spies return. However, in a little twist, today we're going to act out the story of what happened when the spies returned. I'm going to need at least seven actors to join me up front.

[If you have a smaller class, ask a few of the actors to play dual roles. Assign each of the actors one of the following roles: Moses, Joshua, Caleb, God, Spy, Israelite #1, Israelite #2, and Israelites (this can be a few actors or the whole class).
Optional: If you want, you can give each actor a prop: a staff for Moses, sheriff badges for Joshua and Caleb, binoculars for the spy, a stick with crumpled tissue paper on top to hide the face of God in "a cloud of smoke or fire," and tissues for the Israelites.]

SAY: We pick up our story today from the Book of Numbers at the end of chapter 13 and going through chapter 14. It's all about the interaction between and the way they trust in God. Take it away!

[Let the students act out the lesson using the Spy vs. Spy script included in the Student Journals.]

ASK: What stood out to you from this story? What did the spies and the people miss that Joshua and Caleb could see?

ASK: What did you think about God's response and God's interaction with Moses?

REVEAL (10 minutes)

SAY: Over the centuries, Christian writers have noted the wilderness as a theme that occurs throughout the Bible and have found it a fitting metaphor for the times in our lives when we experience emptiness, isolation, and confusion. The Israelites constantly claimed that they wanted to escape the wilderness, but when they were presented with just that opportunity, they revealed that what they actually wanted was the familiarity of Egypt and the illusion of safety. They couldn't trust God to lead them into the unknown. It turns out that the wilderness was exactly what they needed: a time to experience God's support and presence while shedding their romanticized views of Egypt.

SAY: Today's journal questions will help us reflect on our own experiences in the wilderness. Go ahead and open your Student Journals and take the next few minutes to reflect on the questions you find there.

[Allow the students seven or eight minutes to write their answers. When they're finished, ask if anyone wants to share some of their thoughts with the class.]

Journal Questions

1) What does the word "wilderness" bring to mind for you?
2) Have you ever had an experience you would describe as a "wilderness experience"? How would you describe that experience?
3) Have you ever been glad that you had to wait for something you wanted? Why?
4) What do you think about the younger generation having to pay for the older generation's sin alongside them?

BUILD (10-15 minutes)

[Split the students back into their groups from the Sync activity, and assign each group a number from 1 to 3. Each group will be assigned one of the following passages:
Exodus 15:22-26—turning bitter water sweet;
Exodus 17:1-7—water from a rock;
Numbers 21:4-9—the bronze snake's healing power.]

SAY: We're going to continue our dramatic retelling of the Israelites' time in the wilderness by acting out some more scenes from the Books of Exodus and Numbers. This time your group will have five minutes to read the passage you've been assigned and compose your skit. The skit should be a maximum of thirty seconds long. As you compose your skit, keep in mind what the wilderness means to us today, and give your skit a new setting—maybe it's set in Siberia, or outer space. It's up to you. You'll find your passage in your Student Journals.

[After the students have split off into their groups and numbered off, give them five minutes to plan. This activity is more fun if the timing for the skit is strict, so try to stick to the thirty-second time limit. If you have a screen with a countdown clock available, try and make that visible to the students as they perform.]

SAY: Okay, now that you're ready, we're going to give our performances in the order that they're assigned. You'll have thirty seconds to give your performance, and we're going to be really strict about that time limit. If you go over thirty seconds, then everyone in the audience will start yelling, "Cut!" You'll have ten seconds once the last group finishes until the thirty seconds for the next group starts, so be ready when your group is next! Group number one, get set. Go!

[Start the timer. Move quickly through each group. Encourage the students to have fun with the quick turnover. If the pace becomes too stressful for one of the groups, ease off the pressure. This activity is supposed to be a fun and lighthearted way to explore these stories.]

SAY: Okay, great job, everyone! I want everyone to tell me one thing you learned either from the passage you got to perform or one of the other passages you saw acted out.

[Go around and let each student share something they learned.]

AFTER (5 minutes)

[Invite the students to participate in one of these After activities. Send them a reminder during the week.]

Someone Who's Gone Before

SAY: This week ask a teacher, leader, or family member to tell you about a time in the past when they felt like they were in the wilderness—stuck, wandering, confused, or lonely. Share with them a time when you've felt this way.

Ch-ch-ch-changes

SAY: Write a letter to yourself from three years ago about the ways you've grown since then. Alternatively, write a letter to yourself five years in the future about the ways you hope to grow.

Reframing

SAY: This week try to give thanks for two things each time you complain about one thing. Tell a close friend that you're trying to do this so that they can keep you accountable. Finally, post something you're thankful for on social media this week.

PRAYER

SAY: God, we thank you for all the ways you are working when we are unaware of it. Please help us to stay steady when we are in the wilderness and to encourage others when they find themselves there. Amen.

FATH●M

God's Community Cares for the Poor

Summary

Students will learn about what the Book of Deuteronomy has to say about money and the way we treat those who are poor. It's important to show that the law envisions a world where people care for one another because there is plenty to go around.

Overview

- **Sync** the students with ideas about money and scarcity.
- **Tour** through passages in Deuteronomy that illuminate how the Israelites were to use their resources.
- **Reveal** more about how the law encourages us to treat money and other resources.
- **Build** on the principle of tithing by planning a tithe party.
- **After** the lesson, the students will choose an activity that helps bring godly attitudes to their own understanding of money.

Anchor Point

- Deuteronomy 15:10—*Give generously to needy persons. Don't resent giving to them because it is this very thing that will lead to the LORD your God's blessing you in all you do and work at.*

Supplies

- Student Journals
- Way to play music in class
- Posterboard
- Paper
- Markers
- Large quantity of small candy, pennies, or seeds
- Various trinkets for students to "buy"

Parent E-mail

This week's lesson focuses on money and economics in Deuteronomy. This book encourages God's people to operate from a mindset of abundance and trust in God's provision. Here are some ways to help your student think about this highly practical topic:

- Share the details of your family budget with your youth and help them make a budget of their own.
- Help your student choose a charity to make a monthly giving commitment. Consider matching their gift, learning about and praying for the organization together.
- Tell your student about a time when you experienced God's provision.

Leader Notes

Most people have their first job in high school, and regardless of their economic background or class, they begin seriously considering money and economics for the first time as teenagers. Depending on their family situation, many may already have strong feelings about money, budgets, work, saving, and giving. The Book of Deuteronomy can help us all fit our understanding and our feelings about money within the framework of our relationships to others and God.

Theology and Commentary

The Book of Deuteronomy is intended to be read as one long speech from Moses to the new generation of Israelites before they enter the Promised Land. Moses describes the nation's history with God, reiterates the laws that they are to follow in the new land, and impresses upon them the importance of keeping the covenant. The laws laid out generally echo those from Leviticus, but changes in the details reflect the culture and concerns of a new generation of Israelites.

While much of the narrative in the Bible moves along at a fast pace, reading through the laws in the same manner easily leads to confusion and boredom. It's not always clear why they're arranged as they are, and many laws can seem obscure or fussy. Often, several layers of culture, lifestyle, and technology stand between us and the people who wrote and followed them. One of the best ways we can approach these laws is to think of them as a way to envision the holy and God-fearing society that would display God's glory to the surrounding nations. In this way, we come to see connections that are not evident when simply riding straight through.

For example, in Deuteronomy 14 and 15 we see an important value that is woven throughout the law. It is expected that Israel will approach its resources and neighbors with an attitude of abundance. The tithe in chapter 14 is a harvest celebration, and the people are called to bring their first fruits to God in gratitude. Whereas we often think of tithes as a somber duty, Deuteronomy depicts a joyous or even raucous celebration. However, every third year is a year of restraint on behalf of the poor. Deuteronomy's tithe is a cycle of feasting and fasting, both of which should be included in an appropriate response to the abundance of God's provision.

The year of Jubilee (canceled debts) in Deuteronomy 15 likewise encourages the people to hold their possessions loosely and to prioritize the flourishing of their neighbors over material gain. It ensures that no family will be consigned to prison or debt slavery forever simply because they've fallen on hard times. This spirit of the law is clear. The wealthy should care for the poor, even when the cancellation of debt is approaching. This is not a complete lack of accountability; debts and debt slavery still exist. But the law is designed to prevent wealthy people from exploiting the hardships of the poor.

The basic assumption of the law throughout Deuteronomy is that there will always be enough to go around. Even when we think we need to take more to provide for our families and ourselves, we should refrain. If we are in need, God will provide.

Leader Reflection

In the late Middle Ages, debates raged over a topic we would likely find puzzling today: Was it a sin to lend money at interest? The practice became widespread in Europe as wealth and economic opportunities increased, and many were suspicious of the idea. Moreover, they pointed out that this type of lending is prohibited throughout the Bible.

Today, of course, loans and interest rates are simply a part of life. Yet, even though the economic practices that sustain our way of life have changed immensely over time, it's surprising how relatable much of the Bible's direction on money can be. Whether we are farmers in an agricultural economy or software engineers in a technological one, we still struggle to sustain a healthy relationship with money.

The laws in Deuteronomy 14 and 15 make it clear that our relationship with money cannot be properly managed through rules alone, but only by creating a healthy attitude toward wealth and God's provision. Giving to neighbors, therefore, is not an obligatory nuisance, but an occasion for joy and gratitude born out of an understanding that in God's kingdom, there is an abundance to be shared.

Ideas like these challenge the notions of our acquisitive society and idolization of meritocracy. For every Bible verse that requires us to look after our brothers and sisters, there is a message elsewhere telling us that money is scarce, that we earned what we have, and that we can't possibly be responsible for everyone. As you prepare for this lesson, pray that God would fill us with the conviction that abundance is found in sharing and trusting in God to fulfill our needs.

NOTES

SYNC (10 minutes)

High-Energy Option—Broken Bonds Musical Chairs

[Before class, set up a way to play music in class, and recruit a volunteer to start and stop the music.]

SAY: To start today, I need everyone to grab a chair and put it somewhere in the room. There should be a jumble of chairs all over.

[Give everyone a minute to do this. Don't put a chair out for yourself; there should be one less chair than people.]

SAY: We're going to play a version of musical chairs, but with our own rules. Everyone is going to close their eyes, hold hands, and follow me in a line until the music stops. When it stops, open your eyes and find a chair to sit in. The last person standing is out of the game and will sit for the rest of the game in one of the chairs. Everybody ready? Get in line and grab a hand!

[Have the volunteer start and stop the music at random. Lead everyone in a twisting, random path around the room. If you're eliminated, you may need to designate a new leader. Once you have a single winner, congratulate them and have the loser take a seat. Stand in the center of the group.]

SAY: Did you think that game was stressful? I know I did. When there aren't enough resources for everyone, there has to be a loser—and no one wants to be the loser. The competition can even break the bonds of our communities. Today we're going to see that the Bible can help us build a world where there's always enough to go around.

Low-Energy Option—That's the Way the Candy Crumbles

[Before the lesson, set up a "store" in the middle of the circle. On a table, place several small trinkets, and mark them with prices that will be paid in pieces of candy (or seeds or pennies, something small). Examples might include a pencil for two pieces of candy or a notebook for eight pieces of candy.]

[As the students come in, give out candy (or whatever you've chosen as currency) as follows: first student = one, second student = three, third student = five, fourth student = ten, fifth student = twenty-five. Every student after the fifth should get either three or five. This roughly represents the global income distribution. Tell the students to hang on to the candy until the activity starts. Once everyone has arrived, gather in a circle around the store.]

SAY: Before we start our discussion today, I want to give you all the chance to trade in your candy for anything you see here—as long as you can afford it. Go ahead and count how much you have, and we'll start with the person on my left.

[When it's each person's turn, ask them how many pieces they have. Encourage them to make their decisions quickly and move on to the next person. If anyone complains that it's not fair, just shrug and say, "That's just the way it is." Give everyone a chance to buy from the store.]

SAY: I have a question, and I want you all to shout our your answer to my question at the same time on the count of three. How did that situation make you feel? One, two, three!

[Repeat any interesting answers you hear, and ask why someone might feel that way.]

ASK: What did you think about your neighbors having so much more or less than you did?

[Encourage the students to discuss this with one another. If any students interacted by bartering, buying, giving, or sharing candy, ask them why they did that. If not, ask everyone why they didn't try that or try to change the situation.]

SAY: The amounts of candy you all received today roughly reflect the incomes in the world today. You'll see in your Student Journals a chart showing the breakdown of income worldwide. Today we're going to talk about money and poverty, and I want you to keep this activity in mind. Think about what it means to live in a society that's unequal.

TOUR (20 minutes)

[Divide the students into three groups, and assign each group a number. Have paper, posterboard, and markers available for each group.]

SAY: Today we're going to rely on each other to try and understand the Scripture we'll be studying. The chapters we're talking about include a few policies that governed how the Israelites were supposed to handle their money and possessions. As we explored last week, the laws God gave the people exist to show Israel what kind of society they should build to honor God. The law invites them to do certain things to remind them of God's presence in the community. That includes rules on how they should use their money.

SAY: Of course, when we talk about money, we have to realize that the Israelites didn't have bank accounts or paychecks or credit cards. They had grain stores, daily wages, and debt slavery—the practice of selling oneself as a slave when you couldn't pay your debts. These concepts might sound foreign, but ancient Israel struggled with the same questions we do: How should we treat people who are poor? How do we trust God when things don't go as planned? What are money and possessions for?

SAY: When we look closely at the policies we're going to read about today, we can get closer to answering these questions. Each group is going to explain their assigned policy to us through a public service announcement that they create. You can create a poster, act out a commercial, or come up with your own creative spin on how to explain your policy to the group. You'll have about ten minutes to read through the passage in your Student Journal and put together your announcement.

[Assign the groups the following passages:
Group 1—Deuteronomy 14:22-29;
Group 2—Deuteronomy 15:1-6;
Group 3—Deuteronomy 15:7-11.]

[Give the students time to formulate their presentations. As they're working, walk around and ask each group whether they have any questions about the Bible passage. Reconvene the large group after ten minutes.]

SAY: It's time for each group to give their presentations. As you're watching the other groups, jot down something about each policy that's different from the way we usually do things now. Do I have any volunteers to go first?

[Invite the first group up, and then the two following groups. As each group finishes, ask the following questions of them.]

ASK: What is different about your policy from what we're used to in the world today? What attitudes would help a person or a society embrace this practice?

[After all the groups are done, thank them and applaud them for their work.]

REVEAL (5 minutes)

[Let each student choose a partner and split off into pairs.]

SAY: Take a few minutes to think silently about the questions in your Student Journals.

[After a minute or two . . .]

SAY: With your partner, go ahead and discuss your thoughts about these questions. As you discuss, write down your thoughts in the space below each question.

Journal Questions

1) Taking all three of the policies we discussed together, what attitudes do you see present about money and possessions in Deuteronomy?
2) How do these attitudes compare to the messages about money we hear from commercials, political debates, and other parts of society?
3) What do you make of the verses that say "there won't be any poor persons among you" and "poor persons will never disappear from the earth"?

BUILD (10 minutes)

[Have the students stay with their partners from the Reveal section. Have paper and markers available.]

SAY: In Deuteronomy 14, we learned that one of the things that God commands is that the Israelites should set apart ten percent of what they produce and have a feast to celebrate God's presence.

SAY: Even if you have an after-school job, you probably don't make much money. But what about when you have a job as an adult? In the United States, the median household income is just over $50,000 a year. Imagine what kind of party you could throw with $5,000 to celebrate God's presence with you and your neighbors!

SAY: Spend the next ten minutes with your partner and plan a party together that costs $5,000. Once you've planned it, design an invitation for the party. Use the questions in your Student Journal as a guide to be as specific as possible. You can also use your phones to check out Pinterest and Instagram for inspiration.

[Let the students imagine their parties. Travel around to the pairs to ask questions and help them stay on task.]

ASK: Who wants to show us their invitation and tell us about their party?

[Call on pairs to share their ideas.]

AFTER (5 minutes)

[Invite the students to participate in an After activity. Send them a reminder during the week]

Biblical Budgeting

SAY: With a family member, make a budget of your current income that reflects the priorities you see in Deuteronomy. Once you're finished, ask God to help you trust God for the resources you need and to help you give away resources more freely.

Behind the Scenes

SAY: Whenever you buy something this week, think about the people (farmers, factory workers, truckers, stockers, cashiers) who helped bring it to you. Post a note of gratitude on social media to these people whose work goes unseen.

Account Your Blessings

SAY: Over the course of the next week, make a list or take a photo of all your gifts and blessings. Try to take note of at least fifteen things in the next week.

PRAYER

SAY: As we pray, please join in silently with your own praises to God.

God, we give you thanks for the gifts you've given us.

[Leave a few seconds of silence for everyone to give thanks for their own gifts.]

Please help us to trust you for the things we need. Help us to hold our resources loosely and to give generously to needy persons.

[Let everyone add to or affirm this in silence.]

Amen.

Explore More

Be Still

Anchor Point
• Exodus 13:17–14:31

Summary

God guides Israel out of Egypt and through the desert. However, the Israelites still complain and are filled with despair. Moses urges them to greater faith, and God comes through with a spectacular victory over the Egyptians.

Takeaways

• God reminds us not to despair, even when we think our backs are against a wall.
• Even when our enemies seem invincible, God is still bigger and more powerful. God will help us through any ordeal.

Take a Break

Anchor Points
• Exodus 20:8 and Deuteronomy 5:12

Summary

God rested on the seventh day, and we are called to follow God's example. Talk through the implications of following this command even when Israel's neighbors didn't. How would it affect their economy? their social structures? their understanding of God and their purpose in life?

Takeaways

• The Bible envisions a day set aside for worship and rest.
• It is not our work or our productivity that make us valuable to God. We are valuable because God created us in God's image.

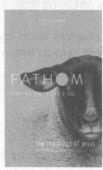

CPSIA information can be obtained
at www.ICGtesting.com
Printed in the USA
JSHW031912010523
41119JS00004B/207